INVESTING REVIVAL

Rebuilding Your Portfolio in 60 Days

Dan Wayne

Copyright © 2023

Table of Contents

INTRODUCTION

In an ever-evolving financial landscape, the art of investing requires adaptability and strategy. "Investing Revival: Rebuilding Your Portfolio in 60 Days" beckons both novice and seasoned investors to embark on a transformative journey. In a world marked by uncertainties, market fluctuations, and technological advancements, this comprehensive guide offers a roadmap to rejuvenate and fortify your investment portfolio within a concise 60-day timeline.

The modern investment sphere demands more than mere luck; it necessitates informed decisions and calculated risks. This guide recognizes that investment is not a one-size-fits-all endeavor, addressing a diverse array of asset classes, risk appetites, and financial goals. Whether you're recovering from market setbacks, seeking to diversify, or starting anew, this resource empowers you to navigate challenges and seize opportunities.

With its holistic approach, "Investing Revival" covers essential aspects, including portfolio assessment, goal definition, strategic planning, risk management, and staying attuned to market trends. From stocks and bonds to real estate and emerging sectors like cryptocurrency, this guide demystifies options, enabling you to make choices aligned with your vision.

In a rapidly changing economic landscape, rebuilding your portfolio is not merely about recovering losses, but about embracing innovation and envisioning a prosperous future. "Investing Revival: Rebuilding Your Portfolio in 60 Days" isn't just a guide – it's a transformative experience equipping you with the tools to navigate the dynamic world of investing and embark on a path towards financial resurgence.

CHAPTER ONE

Assessing Your Starting Point: Building the Foundation for Investment Revival

In the ever-changing world of finance, the key to successful investing lies in a comprehensive understanding of one's current financial standing and investment portfolio. To embark on a journey of revitalizing your investment strategy, it is essential to begin by assessing your starting point. This process involves evaluating your portfolio's performance, recognizing areas in need of improvement, gauging your risk tolerance, defining your financial goals, and establishing an investment timeline. This foundational step paves the way for a well-informed and strategic approach to rebuilding your portfolio within a specified 60-day period.

The Significance of Portfolio Assessment

Portfolio assessment is the cornerstone of investment revival. It entails a thorough analysis of your existing investments, tracking their performance over a defined period. The goal is to identify what's working and what isn't, ensuring that your investment choices align with your financial objectives. By reviewing your portfolio's performance, you gain insights into whether your investments are meeting expectations, outperforming benchmarks, or falling short.

Performance Metrics: Beyond the Surface
When evaluating your portfolio's performance, it's crucial to consider a range of performance metrics. Traditional metrics such as return on investment (ROI) provide a basic overview, but deeper analysis involves examining risk-adjusted returns, volatility, and measures like the Sharpe ratio. This holistic approach paints a clearer picture of how your investments have fared, factoring in the level of risk taken to achieve those returns.

Tracking Diversification and Allocation
Assessing your portfolio also involves evaluating diversification and asset allocation. Diversification across different asset classes, industries, and geographic regions helps mitigate risk. An imbalanced allocation could expose you to unnecessary vulnerabilities. Analyzing how your assets are distributed within your portfolio allows you to identify over-concentration in a particular sector or asset type.

Identifying Areas for Improvement

Portfolio assessment is not just about celebrating successes; it's equally about recognizing areas that need improvement. Some investments might consistently underperform, while others may be too risky for your risk tolerance level. Perhaps certain assets no longer align with your long-term objectives. By identifying these weak points, you can strategize how to address them during the revival process.

Cutting Losses and Letting Go
During the assessment, you might come across investments that are consistently underperforming or no longer align with your investment goals. It's important to evaluate whether holding onto such investments is detrimental to your overall portfolio performance. Sometimes, cutting your losses and selling off underperforming assets can free up capital to be allocated to more promising opportunities.

Realigning with Objectives
Investment goals can evolve over time due to changes in personal circumstances, economic conditions, or shifts in market trends. Review your initial investment objectives and consider whether they remain relevant. If your goals have changed, it

might be time to realign your portfolio accordingly. This could involve adjusting your asset allocation, risk tolerance, and investment horizon.

Gauging Risk Tolerance

Understanding your risk tolerance is a critical step in the assessment process. Risk tolerance refers to your comfort level with the fluctuations in the value of your investments. It's influenced by various factors, including your financial goals, time horizon, and emotional response to market volatility.

Risk Tolerance Questionnaires
Several tools and questionnaires are available to help you gauge your risk tolerance. These assessments typically ask about your investment objectives, time horizon, willingness to take risks, and reaction to potential losses. The results provide a numerical score that reflects your risk tolerance level, which can guide your investment decisions.

Balancing Risk and Reward
Assessing your risk tolerance isn't solely about avoiding risk; it's about finding the balance between risk and potential reward. A high-risk investment might offer substantial returns, but it could also result in significant losses. On the other hand, overly conservative investments might not yield the

desired growth. By aligning your risk tolerance with your investment goals, you can create a portfolio that strikes the right balance for your individual circumstances.

Defining Financial Goals

Investment without clear financial goals is like embarking on a journey without a destination. Defining your financial goals is a crucial aspect of assessing your starting point. Your goals provide the roadmap for your investment strategy, guiding the types of investments you choose and the level of risk you're willing to accept.

Short-Term vs. Long-Term Goals

Financial goals can be categorized as short-term, medium-term, or long-term. Short-term goals might include saving for a vacation or purchasing a new vehicle. Medium-term goals could involve funding a child's education or buying a home. Long-term goals often revolve around retirement planning or building generational wealth. Each category of goal requires a different investment approach to ensure the appropriate level of risk and return.

SMART Goal Framework

To make your financial goals actionable, they should adhere to the SMART framework – Specific, Measurable, Achievable, Relevant, and Time-bound. This structure ensures that your goals are well-defined, quantifiable, realistic, aligned with your aspirations, and bound by a specific timeframe.

Establishing an Investment Timeline

Time is a critical factor in investing. Your investment timeline refers to the period over which you plan to achieve your financial goals. It plays a pivotal role in determining your asset allocation and risk tolerance. Investments aimed at short-term goals might prioritize liquidity and stability, while long-term goals can accommodate a more aggressive approach.

Matching Investments to Timelines
Investments are often classified as short-term, intermediate-term, or long-term based on their expected holding periods. Cash equivalents and stable assets are suitable for short-term goals, while growth-oriented assets like stocks can align with long-term objectives. By aligning your investments with their corresponding timelines, you can maximize the potential for achieving your goals.

Conclusion

Assessing your starting point is the cornerstone of the investment revival process. By evaluating your portfolio's performance, recognizing areas for improvement, gauging your risk tolerance, defining your financial goals, and establishing an investment timeline, you lay a solid foundation for the journey ahead. Armed with insights into your current financial standing, you're better equipped to make informed decisions, allocate resources effectively, and navigate the intricate landscape of investing. This introspective and analytical approach sets the stage for the subsequent chapters of "Investing Revival," where you'll delve into crafting a strategic investment strategy, diversifying your portfolio, managing risks, and ultimately, revitalizing your investments within the span of 60 days.

CHAPTER TWO

Defining Your Investment Strategy: Paving the Path to Financial Success

In the intricate world of investment, success is not solely determined by chance; rather, it stems from a well-defined and carefully crafted investment strategy. To embark on a journey of financial prosperity, it's imperative to delineate a clear investment strategy that resonates with your objectives and risk tolerance. This entails understanding various investment approaches, aligning them with your financial goals, and molding your investment path accordingly. This chapter delves into the art of defining your investment strategy, exploring approaches such as value investing, growth investing, and income-focused strategies, and underscores the significance of harmonizing these strategies with your unique financial circumstances.

Unveiling the Essence of Investment Strategy

An investment strategy serves as the blueprint for navigating the complex world of financial markets. It provides a structured framework for making informed decisions, managing risk, and maximizing returns. Defining your investment strategy is akin to setting the course of a ship in a vast ocean – it steers your investments toward a predetermined destination rather than drifting aimlessly.

The Role of Alignment
A successful investment strategy is one that aligns seamlessly with your financial aspirations, risk appetite, and time horizon. It encapsulates your personalized goals and preferences, shaping your investment decisions to resonate with your unique circumstances. Without this alignment, your strategy can lead to dissonance between your objectives and your investment actions.

Exploring Investment Approaches

Investment strategies can be broadly categorized into several approaches, each offering distinct benefits and challenges. Exploring these approaches allows you to determine which one resonates most with your financial goals and risk profile.

Value Investing
Value investing revolves around identifying undervalued assets that are trading below their intrinsic value. Investors who embrace this approach seek out opportunities where the market has underestimated an asset's true worth. The aim is to buy assets at a discount and wait for the

market to correct itself, resulting in potential long-term gains. Value investing is often associated with the timeless wisdom of Benjamin Graham and his disciple Warren Buffett.

Growth Investing
Growth investing, as the name suggests, focuses on investing in companies with high growth potential. Investors attracted to this approach prioritize capital appreciation over immediate income. These companies typically reinvest their profits into expanding operations, increasing market share, and innovating. Growth investing requires a keen eye for identifying businesses poised for rapid expansion and a tolerance for higher volatility.

Income-Focused Strategies
Income-focused strategies prioritize generating consistent income from investments. This approach is particularly appealing to investors seeking regular cash flow, such as retirees. Dividend stocks, bonds, real estate investment trusts (REITs), and other income-generating assets are popular choices within this strategy. The challenge lies in balancing income generation with capital preservation and growth.

Passive vs. Active Investing

Within the realm of investment strategies, there's also a distinction between passive and active approaches. Passive investing involves tracking a market index or using exchange-traded funds (ETFs) to mirror the market's performance. This strategy is often associated with lower fees and a long-term outlook. Active investing, on the other hand, entails selecting individual investments with the aim of outperforming the market. It requires more hands-on research and decision-making.

Tailoring Your Strategy to Your Goals

Defining your investment strategy isn't a one-size-fits-all endeavor. To ensure its effectiveness, you must tailor it to your unique financial goals and circumstances. Consider the following factors when aligning your strategy:

Time Horizon

The time horizon of your investment goals heavily influences your strategy. Short-term goals may necessitate a more conservative approach with an emphasis on capital preservation. In contrast, long-term goals could accommodate a more aggressive strategy to potentially benefit from higher growth opportunities.

Risk Tolerance

Your risk tolerance is a pivotal element in shaping your investment strategy. It determines the level of volatility you're comfortable with and guides the allocation of assets in your portfolio. A risk-averse investor might lean toward income-focused strategies, while a risk-taker might gravitate toward growth-oriented investments.

Financial Goals

Each financial goal requires a unique investment strategy. Funding a child's education, buying a home, or retiring comfortably all demand different approaches. Defining your goals with the SMART framework – Specific, Measurable, Achievable, Relevant, and Time-bound – aids in crafting an investment strategy tailored to their fulfillment.

Flexibility and Adaptability

The financial landscape is dynamic, and your investment strategy should have room for adaptability. Regularly reviewing and adjusting your strategy in response to market shifts, economic conditions, and personal circumstances is essential for long-term success.

The Holistic Approach: Blending Strategies

While each investment approach has its merits, it's important to recognize that a holistic strategy might involve blending multiple approaches to create a diversified portfolio. A well-rounded portfolio may encompass a mix of value and growth stocks, income-generating assets, and potentially alternative investments like real estate or commodities.

The Power of Diversification
Diversification is a cornerstone of successful investing. By spreading your investments across different asset classes and sectors, you reduce the impact of a single poor-performing investment on your overall portfolio. Diversification can help manage risk while still offering exposure to potential growth.

Conclusion

Defining your investment strategy is an art that involves harmonizing your financial objectives, risk tolerance, and investment approaches. By exploring value investing, growth investing, income-focused strategies, and considering passive versus active investing, you gain insights into the diverse avenues available. The true essence lies in tailoring these approaches to your goals and circumstances, forging a strategy that not only guides your investment decisions but also paves the path to financial success. As you progress through the subsequent chapters of "Investing Revival," armed with a well-defined strategy, you'll embark on a journey of portfolio revitalization that aligns with your aspirations and redefines your financial trajectory.

CHAPTER THREE

Portfolio Diversification and Asset Allocation: Managing Risk and Seizing Opportunities

In the realm of investment, the old adage "Don't put all your eggs in one basket" holds true as a guiding principle. Portfolio diversification and asset allocation are fundamental strategies that empower investors to navigate the complex landscape of financial markets. By spreading investments across various asset classes, sectors, and geographical regions, investors can mitigate risk, enhance returns, and seize opportunities that align with their financial goals. This chapter delves into the significance of portfolio diversification and effective asset allocation, highlighting their role in managing risk, capturing potential gains, and creating a resilient investment portfolio.

Unveiling the Power of Portfolio Diversification

Portfolio diversification is a strategy that aims to reduce risk by investing in a variety of assets that perform differently under various market conditions. The core principle is to avoid over-concentration in a single investment, sector, or asset class, thereby minimizing the impact of poor performance in any one area. Instead of placing all investments in a single "basket," diversification spreads them across multiple "baskets."

The Risk-Return Tradeoff
Diversification hinges on the risk-return tradeoff, which stipulates that there's a balance between risk and potential return. While riskier investments may offer higher returns, they also come with greater volatility and potential for losses. By diversifying, investors can achieve a mix of assets that collectively balance risk and return, creating a smoother and more predictable investment journey.

Asset Classes and Sectors
Diversification extends to various asset classes, including stocks, bonds, real estate, commodities, and alternative investments. It also encompasses different sectors within the market, such as technology, healthcare, finance, and energy. A diversified portfolio avoids putting too much emphasis on a single sector, minimizing the impact of sector-specific downturns.

The Art of Effective Asset Allocation

Asset allocation is the process of determining the distribution of investments among different asset classes. This strategy is rooted in the understanding that each asset class has a unique risk and return profile. Effective asset allocation considers an investor's risk tolerance, investment goals, and time horizon.

Strategic vs. Tactical Asset Allocation
There are two main approaches to asset allocation: strategic and tactical. Strategic asset allocation involves establishing a predetermined mix of assets based on long-term goals and risk tolerance. Tactical asset allocation, on the other hand, involves adjusting the portfolio's asset allocation in response to short-term market fluctuations. Both approaches have their merits, and the choice depends on an investor's preferences and objectives.

The Importance of Rebalancing
As markets fluctuate, the initial asset allocation of a portfolio can shift over time. This is where portfolio rebalancing comes into play. Rebalancing involves periodically readjusting the asset allocation to restore it to the original intended percentages. This practice ensures that the risk-reward balance of the portfolio remains aligned with an investor's goals, preventing overexposure to specific assets.

The Role of Geographical Diversification

Geographical diversification extends beyond asset classes and sectors to encompass different regions and countries. Investing solely in one country's market exposes a portfolio to the economic and political risks of that country. Geographical diversification aims to reduce this risk by spreading investments across various global markets.

Benefits of Global Exposure
Different regions experience varying economic cycles, political events, and market trends. By diversifying geographically, investors can tap into growth opportunities and mitigate the impact of localized economic downturns. Furthermore, international exposure can provide exposure to industries and sectors that may not be prevalent in domestic markets.

Exchange Rates and Currency Risk
Geographical diversification also introduces currency risk. Fluctuations in exchange rates can impact the value of international investments when converted back to the investor's home currency. Investors should consider the potential effects of currency fluctuations and explore strategies to manage this risk.

Building a Diversified Portfolio

Building a diversified portfolio involves thoughtful consideration of asset allocation and selection. The process requires a comprehensive understanding of an investor's risk tolerance, financial goals, and investment horizon. Here's a step-by-step guide:

Step 1: Determine Your Risk Tolerance
Assess your risk tolerance using tools and questionnaires. This will guide the level of risk you're comfortable taking on in your portfolio.

Step 2: Set Your Investment Goals
Define your investment goals with the SMART framework. This will help you establish clear objectives that align with your risk tolerance and time horizon.

Step 3: Choose Asset Classes
Select a mix of asset classes that align with your risk tolerance and goals. Consider a combination of stocks, bonds, real estate, and potentially alternative investments.

Step 4: Allocate Assets
Allocate a percentage of your portfolio to each chosen asset class. Strategic asset allocation should

reflect your long-term goals, while tactical adjustments can address short-term market trends.

Step 5: Rebalance Periodically
Monitor your portfolio's performance and periodically rebalance it to maintain the intended asset allocation. Rebalancing ensures that your portfolio's risk profile remains in line with your goals.

Achieving Resilience and Opportunity

Portfolio diversification and effective asset allocation are not only risk-management tools but also avenues for capturing growth opportunities. By diversifying across asset classes, sectors, and geographical regions, investors position themselves to weather market storms and capitalize on market upswings. This chapter underscores the pivotal role of a well-diversified portfolio and strategic asset allocation in building a resilient investment strategy that stands the test of time. As you proceed through the subsequent chapters of "Investing Revival," armed with the wisdom of diversification, you'll find yourself better equipped to navigate the complexities of financial markets and embark on a journey of portfolio revitalization.

CHAPTER FOUR

Strategic Investment Selection: Navigating the Landscape of Investment Vehicles

In the dynamic world of finance, where myriad investment vehicles beckon, the art of strategic investment selection reigns supreme. Crafting a well-rounded and diversified portfolio requires astute decision-making, fueled by thorough research, due diligence, and a clear alignment with your investment strategy. This chapter delves into the multifaceted realm of investment vehicles, encompassing stocks, bonds, real estate, commodities, and emerging technologies. It unravels the process of effective investment selection, providing insights into the importance of research, risk assessment, and the delicate balance between potential returns and inherent risks.

The Array of Investment Vehicles

The investment landscape brims with a variety of vehicles, each offering unique opportunities, risk profiles, and potential rewards. Exploring different investment vehicles allows you to tailor your portfolio to align with your financial goals and risk tolerance.

Stocks: Ownership in Companies
Stocks represent ownership in a company and provide investors with a claim on its assets and earnings. Publicly traded stocks are listed on exchanges, offering liquidity and the potential for capital appreciation. They encompass various sectors and industries, enabling investors to tap into different areas of the economy.

Bonds: Fixed-Income Securities
Bonds are fixed-income securities that represent loans made by investors to entities such as governments or corporations. In exchange for the loan, bondholders receive regular interest payments and the return of the principal at maturity. Bonds are often favored for their income-generating potential and relative stability compared to stocks.

Real Estate: Tangible Assets
Real estate investments encompass properties such as residential, commercial, and industrial real estate. Real estate offers the potential for rental income and capital appreciation. It can serve as a hedge against inflation and provides diversification beyond traditional financial assets.

Commodities: Physical Goods

Commodities include physical goods such as gold, oil, agricultural products, and metals. Investing in commodities can provide exposure to asset classes that move independently of traditional financial markets. Commodities can act as a hedge against inflation and currency fluctuations.

Emerging Technologies: Innovation and Disruption

Investing in emerging technologies, such as artificial intelligence, blockchain, and renewable energy, offers exposure to industries poised for rapid growth and innovation. While potentially lucrative, these investments often come with higher volatility and risks associated with technological advancements.

The Art of Thorough Research

Effective investment selection is founded on rigorous research. Comprehensive due diligence allows you to evaluate the potential risks and rewards of each investment vehicle, enabling informed decision-making aligned with your investment strategy.

Analyzing Financials
For stocks and bonds, delving into the financial health of the issuing entity is paramount. Analyze financial statements, earnings reports, and debt levels to assess stability, growth prospects, and the ability to meet financial obligations.

Understanding Real Estate Markets
When considering real estate investments, understanding local market trends, property values, rental demand, and potential cash flow is crucial. Conduct market research and property evaluations to make informed decisions.

Comprehending Commodities Markets
Commodities investments require insight into supply and demand dynamics, geopolitical influences, and macroeconomic trends. Stay attuned to factors that impact commodity prices and market volatility.

Evaluating Emerging Technologies
Investing in emerging technologies demands a grasp of the industry landscape, competitive positioning, regulatory considerations, and potential barriers to adoption. Evaluate the technological innovation and long-term viability of the investment.

The Balancing Act: Risk and Return

Investment selection entails striking a delicate balance between potential returns and inherent risks. Different investment vehicles offer varying levels of risk and reward, and your choice should align with your risk tolerance and financial goals.

Risk Assessment
Assessing risk involves evaluating factors such as volatility, liquidity, market conditions, and external influences. Diversification across different investment vehicles can mitigate risk by spreading exposure.

Return Potential
While higher returns are attractive, they often come with increased risk. Understand the historical performance of each investment vehicle and set realistic expectations for returns that align with your strategy.

Time Horizon
The time horizon of your investment goals influences the choice of investment vehicle. Short-term goals may prioritize liquidity and

stability, while long-term goals can accommodate higher-risk, higher-return options.

Constructing a Diversified Portfolio

A well-constructed portfolio leverages the strengths of various investment vehicles to achieve diversification and optimize risk-reward tradeoffs. Consider the following steps when constructing your portfolio:

Step 1: Define Your Asset Allocation
Based on your risk tolerance and goals, allocate a percentage of your portfolio to each asset class, including stocks, bonds, real estate, and commodities.

Step 2: Research Specific Investments
Within each asset class, research specific investments that align with your strategy. Evaluate the track record, financial health, and growth potential of companies or entities.

Step 3: Assess Risk and Potential Returns
Evaluate the risk and return profiles of each investment option. Consider historical performance, market conditions, and external factors that could impact future returns.

Step 4: Achieve Diversification
Construct a portfolio that achieves diversification across different investment vehicles. This spreads risk and optimizes returns by capturing opportunities in various market segments.

Conclusion
Strategic investment selection is an art that requires a blend of research, due diligence, and alignment with your investment strategy. Exploring diverse investment vehicles – stocks, bonds, real estate, commodities, and emerging technologies – empowers you to craft a well-rounded portfolio that aligns with your financial goals and risk tolerance. As you proceed through the subsequent chapters of "Investing Revival," armed with insights into effective investment selection, you'll navigate the complexities of financial markets and embark on a journey of portfolio revitalization that's poised for success.

CHAPTER FIVE

Risk Management Techniques: Safeguarding Your Portfolio Amid Market Volatility

In the ever-fluctuating landscape of finance, the art of investing extends beyond profit-seeking to encompass a critical aspect: risk management. As investors navigate the highs and lows of markets, understanding and applying effective risk management techniques become imperative to protect and fortify their portfolios. This chapter delves into the realm of risk management, unraveling strategies such as hedging, stop-loss orders, and prudent position sizing. By mastering these techniques, investors can shield their investments from potential downturns, minimize losses, and foster long-term financial resilience.

The Crucial Role of Risk Management

Risk management is a proactive approach to safeguarding your investments against unforeseen events and market fluctuations. While risk is an inherent part of investing, prudent risk management aims to mitigate its impact and create a buffer against potential losses.

The Importance of Balance

Effective risk management strikes a balance between risk and reward. It involves making calculated decisions that align with your risk tolerance while optimizing the potential for returns. This balance allows investors to navigate uncertainty without exposing themselves to excessive risk.

The Spectrum of Risk

Risk takes various forms in investing – market risk, credit risk, liquidity risk, and more. While risk can't be eliminated entirely, it can be managed strategically to protect against adverse outcomes.

Hedging: Guarding Against Downside Risk

Hedging is a risk management technique that involves using financial instruments to offset potential losses in your portfolio. It's akin to buying insurance for your investments.

Derivative Instruments

Derivative instruments such as options and futures contracts are common tools for hedging. Put options, for instance, give you the right to sell a security at a predetermined price within a specific timeframe. If the security's value declines, the put option can offset the losses.

Diversification as a Form of Hedging
Diversification, a cornerstone of risk management, can also be seen as a form of hedging. By spreading investments across different asset classes and sectors, you reduce the impact of poor performance in any single investment.

Utilizing Stop-Loss Orders

A stop-loss order is a powerful tool to limit potential losses in your portfolio. It involves setting a predetermined price at which a security will be sold, automatically executing the sale if the security's price reaches or falls below that level.

Types of Stop-Loss Orders
Different types of stop-loss orders cater to varying risk tolerances and market conditions. A traditional stop-loss order becomes a market order when the security's price hits the specified level. A trailing stop-loss order, however, adjusts as the security's price increases, helping you lock in profits while still guarding against downside risk.

Setting Appropriate Stop-Loss Levels
Setting stop-loss levels requires careful consideration of your risk tolerance and the historical volatility of the security. Setting the

stop-loss too close to the current price may result in premature selling, while setting it too far might expose you to larger losses.

Prudent Position Sizing: Controlling Exposure

Position sizing refers to determining the amount of capital allocated to a specific investment. Proper position sizing not only optimizes potential returns but also limits the impact of losses on your portfolio.

Percentage of Portfolio Method
One common approach to position sizing is allocating a specific percentage of your portfolio's total value to each investment. This ensures that no single investment has an outsized impact on your overall portfolio.

Risk-Adjusted Position Sizing
Risk-adjusted position sizing takes into account the risk of each investment relative to your overall portfolio. Investments with higher risk may be allocated a smaller portion of your capital, while more stable investments receive a larger allocation.

Staying Informed: Monitoring and Adapting

Risk management is an ongoing process that requires vigilance and adaptation to changing market conditions. Staying informed about market trends, economic indicators, and geopolitical events empowers you to make timely decisions to safeguard your portfolio.

Regular Portfolio Monitoring
Regularly monitoring your portfolio's performance and reviewing your risk management strategies allows you to detect early warning signs and make necessary adjustments.

Flexibility in Risk Management
Risk management strategies should remain flexible to accommodate market shifts and unexpected developments. Being open to adjusting your strategies in response to new information is crucial for effective risk management.

Balancing Risk and Reward

Investment success is predicated on striking a delicate balance between risk and reward. Risk management techniques empower investors to safeguard their portfolios while still capturing potential gains.

Aligning Risk Management with Investment Strategy

Your risk management approach should be aligned with your overall investment strategy. Conservative investors might emphasize hedging and stricter position sizing, while more aggressive investors might employ stop-loss orders as they seek higher returns.

Risk and Return Expectations

Understanding the relationship between risk and return is essential. While risk management can protect against losses, it can also limit potential gains. Striking the right balance ensures that your portfolio aligns with your financial goals.

Conclusion

Risk management techniques are the shields that protect your investments from the unpredictability of financial markets. By mastering strategies such as hedging, employing stop-loss orders, and practicing prudent position sizing, you equip yourself to weather downturns and fortify your portfolio's resilience. As you navigate the chapters of "Investing Revival," armed with the wisdom of risk management, you'll embark on a journey of portfolio revitalization that's marked by informed decision-making, adaptive strategies, and a commitment to achieving long-term financial success.

CHAPTER SIX

Monitoring and Adjusting Your Portfolio: Navigating the Dynamic Seas of Investing

In the ever-evolving realm of finance, investing is a dynamic journey that demands constant vigilance and adaptability. The process doesn't end once you've crafted your investment strategy and assembled your portfolio; rather, it enters a phase of ongoing monitoring and adjustment. This chapter explores the vital significance of actively monitoring your portfolio, adapting to changing market conditions, and recognizing the right moments to make adjustments and rebalance. By embracing these practices, you empower yourself to navigate the intricate seas of investing, ensuring that your portfolio remains aligned with your objectives and resilient in the face of uncertainty.

The Imperative of Ongoing Monitoring

Portfolio monitoring is a proactive practice that involves regularly assessing the performance of your investments and evaluating their alignment with your goals and risk tolerance. Ongoing monitoring allows you to detect shifts, seize opportunities, and address potential risks before they escalate.

Staying Informed
Staying informed about market trends, economic indicators, geopolitical developments, and changes within industries is pivotal. Regularly reading financial news, reports, and analysis provides the information needed to make informed decisions.

Recognizing Changing Conditions
Markets are dynamic, with conditions that can change rapidly. Monitoring your portfolio enables you to recognize shifts in market sentiment, emerging trends, and potential disruptors that might impact your investments.

Adaptation to Changing Market Conditions

Adapting to changing market conditions is an essential skill for investors. Market volatility, economic fluctuations, and technological advancements necessitate a nimble approach to investment management.

Embracing Flexibility
Being open to adjustments and changes in your investment strategy is crucial. A rigid approach that doesn't adapt to changing circumstances might lead to missed opportunities or unanticipated losses.

Navigating Volatility
Volatility is a characteristic of financial markets. By embracing a long-term perspective and avoiding reactionary decisions during periods of high volatility, you position yourself for more favorable outcomes.

Recognizing the Need for Adjustments

As market conditions evolve, so too should your portfolio. Recognizing the need for adjustments involves evaluating the performance of your investments, risk exposure, and whether your original strategy remains aligned with your goals.

Assessing Investment Performance
Regularly assess the performance of each investment within your portfolio. Identify underperforming assets and evaluate whether they still hold potential or if it's time to consider alternatives.

Reassessing Risk Exposure
Market conditions can influence the risk profile of your portfolio. As risk levels change, reassess the alignment of your portfolio with your risk tolerance and make adjustments as needed.

The Art of Portfolio Rebalancing

Portfolio rebalancing is the process of readjusting the allocation of your investments to maintain the desired asset allocation. This practice ensures that your portfolio remains aligned with your long-term goals and risk tolerance.

Frequency of Rebalancing
The frequency of rebalancing depends on your investment strategy and market conditions. Some investors rebalance annually, while others do so quarterly or in response to significant market shifts.

Maintaining Diversification
Rebalancing helps maintain the desired diversification of your portfolio. If one asset class experiences significant growth, it might become overrepresented in your portfolio, skewing your risk-reward balance.

Methodologies for Rebalancing
Different methodologies exist for rebalancing. The most common involve either allocating new investments to underrepresented asset classes or selling overrepresented assets to reallocate capital.

Recognizing Warning Signs

Monitoring your portfolio enables you to recognize warning signs that might necessitate adjustments. These signs can include changes in market trends, economic indicators, and shifts within specific industries.

Economic Indicators
Pay attention to economic indicators such as GDP growth, inflation rates, and unemployment figures. These indicators provide insights into the overall health of the economy.

Industry-Specific Developments
Industry-specific developments, such as regulatory changes or disruptive technologies, can impact the performance of certain investments. Stay informed about developments within the sectors in which you're invested.

The Wisdom of Patience and Prudence

While adapting and adjusting your portfolio is essential, it's equally important to exercise patience and prudence. Avoid making impulsive decisions based on short-term market fluctuations.

A Long-Term Perspective
Maintain a long-term perspective on your investments. Short-term volatility should be viewed within the context of your overarching financial goals.

Seek Professional Advice
If you're uncertain about when or how to adjust your portfolio, seeking advice from financial professionals can provide valuable insights. Financial advisors can help you navigate complex decisions and align your portfolio with your objectives.

Conclusion

Monitoring and adjusting your portfolio are integral to the journey of investing. By actively staying informed, adapting to changing market conditions, recognizing the need for adjustments, and engaging in portfolio rebalancing, you ensure that your investment strategy remains aligned with your goals and risk tolerance. As you proceed through the chapters of "Investing Revival," armed with the wisdom of ongoing portfolio management, you'll embark on a journey of portfolio revitalization marked by informed decisions, adaptive strategies, and a commitment to achieving lasting financial success.

CHAPTER SEVEN

Staying Informed and Future Trends: Navigating the Path to Tomorrow's Opportunities

In the ever-evolving landscape of finance, staying informed about market trends and future opportunities is not just an advantage; it's a necessity. The ability to anticipate and adapt to emerging trends is instrumental in making informed investment decisions and positioning your portfolio for success. This chapter delves into the methods of staying informed about market dynamics and explores the potential impact of future trends on your investment portfolio. From sustainable investing to technological advancements and geopolitical shifts, understanding these trends equips you to navigate the path to tomorrow's opportunities.

The Power of Staying Informed

Staying informed about market trends and developments is a fundamental aspect of successful investing. Being well-versed in current events, economic indicators, and emerging opportunities empowers you to make timely and well-informed decisions.

News and Financial Media

Regularly consuming news from reputable sources and financial media outlets keeps you updated on market trends, economic data releases, corporate earnings reports, and geopolitical developments that can impact your investments.

Industry Reports and Analysis

Industry-specific reports and analysis provide insights into sector trends, competitive dynamics, and potential growth areas. These reports can help you identify investment opportunities within specific industries.

Financial Education

Invest in your financial education by reading books, attending seminars, and participating in online courses. This empowers you to understand complex financial concepts and make more informed decisions.

Embracing Technological Resources

In the digital age, technology offers a wealth of resources to enhance your knowledge and stay informed about market trends. Utilizing technology can provide real-time insights and access to a vast repository of financial data.

Financial News Apps
Mobile apps provide instant access to breaking news, market data, and financial analysis. You can receive notifications about significant market developments and stay updated on the go.

Investment Platforms
Online investment platforms often offer tools for tracking portfolio performance, analyzing market trends, and accessing research reports. These platforms enable you to monitor your investments and make informed decisions.

Data Analytics and Visualization
Data analytics tools can help you analyze historical data, identify patterns, and visualize trends. These insights can inform your investment strategies and guide decision-making.

Anticipating Future Trends

As you stay informed about current market trends, it's equally important to anticipate future trends that could shape the investment landscape. Identifying and understanding these trends positions your portfolio for long-term success.

Sustainable Investing

Sustainable investing, also known as ESG (Environmental, Social, and Governance) investing, focuses on companies that prioritize environmental sustainability, social responsibility, and ethical governance practices. This trend reflects a growing awareness of the impact of businesses on the world and aims to align investments with values.

Technological Advancements

Technological advancements, including artificial intelligence, blockchain, and renewable energy innovations, are reshaping industries and creating new investment opportunities. Understanding these technologies can help you identify companies poised for growth.

Geopolitical Shifts

Geopolitical events, such as trade agreements, international conflicts, and policy changes, can have far-reaching effects on global markets. Monitoring geopolitical developments helps you anticipate potential market volatility and adjust your investment strategies accordingly.

Demographic Changes

Demographic shifts, such as changing population demographics and generational preferences, influence consumer behavior and market dynamics. Identifying these changes can help you target investments aligned with evolving trends.

Impact on Your Portfolio

Future trends have the potential to impact your investment portfolio in various ways. Recognizing these impacts allows you to proactively adjust your strategy and seize opportunities.

Risk and Opportunity Assessment
Evaluate how future trends align with your risk tolerance and investment goals. Some trends might present lucrative opportunities, while others could introduce new risks.

Portfolio Diversification
Incorporating investments that align with future trends can enhance the diversification of your portfolio. A diversified portfolio reduces concentration risk and positions you to benefit from various growth areas.

Long-Term Performance
Investing in alignment with future trends can contribute to long-term portfolio performance. Companies that adapt to and capitalize on emerging trends may experience sustained growth over time.

Adaptation and Agility

Successfully navigating future trends requires adaptability and agility in your investment approach. A rigid strategy that doesn't respond to changing conditions could hinder your ability to capitalize on emerging opportunities.

Regular Portfolio Review
Regularly reviewing your portfolio's alignment with emerging trends allows you to make necessary adjustments. Consider whether your investments are well-positioned to benefit from or withstand the impacts of these trends.

Evaluating Investment Thesis
As trends evolve, reevaluate your investment thesis for each holding. Consider whether the original reasons for investing remain valid or if adjustments are needed based on changing market dynamics.

Seizing Tomorrow's Opportunities

Staying informed about market trends and anticipating future developments positions you to seize tomorrow's opportunities and navigate potential challenges.

Active Learning and Engagement
Maintain an attitude of active learning and engagement with the financial world. Attend seminars, webinars, and conferences to hear from experts and stay updated on the latest insights.

Networking and Discussion
Engage in discussions with fellow investors, financial professionals, and industry experts. Networking can provide different perspectives and insights that inform your investment decisions.

Conclusion

Staying informed about market trends and anticipating future developments is a cornerstone of successful investing. By employing a combination of traditional and technological resources, understanding the potential impacts of future trends, and adapting your investment strategies accordingly, you position your portfolio to thrive amidst evolving market conditions. As you continue through the chapters of "Investing Revival," armed with the wisdom of staying informed and anticipating trends, you'll embark on a journey of portfolio revitalization that's marked by informed decision-making, adaptability, and a proactive pursuit of tomorrow's opportunities.

www.ingramcontent.com/pod-product-compliance
Lightning Source LLC
Chambersburg PA
CBHW071108260726
48661CB00006B/2542